Free Money Now!
Volume I:
Pocketbook Magic

Ben Prusinski

DEDICATION

I wish to thank my parents and good friends for all of their wonderful support and encouragement. Last but most important I wish to dedicate to readers who seek financial independence by this guide.

CONTENTS

Disclaimer: This book is for educational purposes only and is not legal advice. For financial, accounting or legal advice consult these professionals.

1 FIRST STEPS

Dear reader:

Welcome to learning about money secrets, your personal roadmap to saving big and free money! Now at this point, you are wondering how is free money possible by reading this book? Is it a scam or come on? Everyday we see frauds perpetrated that promise easy riches and quick wealth. Well please rest assured my friends this book is the genuine real deal and not a scam.

If you follow my steps in this book then you will double the value paid for the book. Simple as that. Last year when I was experimenting with these money saving tips, I saved **thousands of dollars at no cost**! Yes, that is fact.

However, it takes a bit of discipline and common sense. A trait sorely lacking in many folks these days. How often do we see people run out to the car dealer to overpay for a new or used car? They buy crap they don't need at Walmart and stores. I hear stories of youngsters who want to be hip and cool at be seen places and nightspots dropping $500-$1000 bar tabs at VIP tables to brag about bottle service. What nonsense! Then they end up broke and whine about no money for anything. Folks wonder why I can drive a nice car. Well I don't waste money. Join me and in this brief voyage you will learn some quick win GUARANTEED tips to save thousands of dollars each year. With the global economic meltdown and never ended cycles of recessions, you most likely want to learn these insider tricks and tips on how to cut expenses and get money back each day and each week.

Ingredients Required for Free Money to Work Magic

In order for you to be successful and achieve these amazing benefits you must first assemble the required ingredients for the recipes and tools to make it work. Just like a skilled artist or talented professional athlete, you need the right stuff to be successful in gaining free money at no risk.

First off, open a bank savings and checking account if you already do not have one. Check your credit report for errors and find out what your FICO score is before moving forward. I will explain why in a little while. If you discover that your credit sucks or FICO score is low under 500, then you have some home work to do before moving forward. I recommend negotiating with creditors to have negative accounts removed from each of the three credit reporting agencies. Establish at least one positive credit card account and pay the balance off in full. You will thank me sooner than later.

For credit reporting, I recommend the website below:
https://www.annualcreditreport.com/index.action

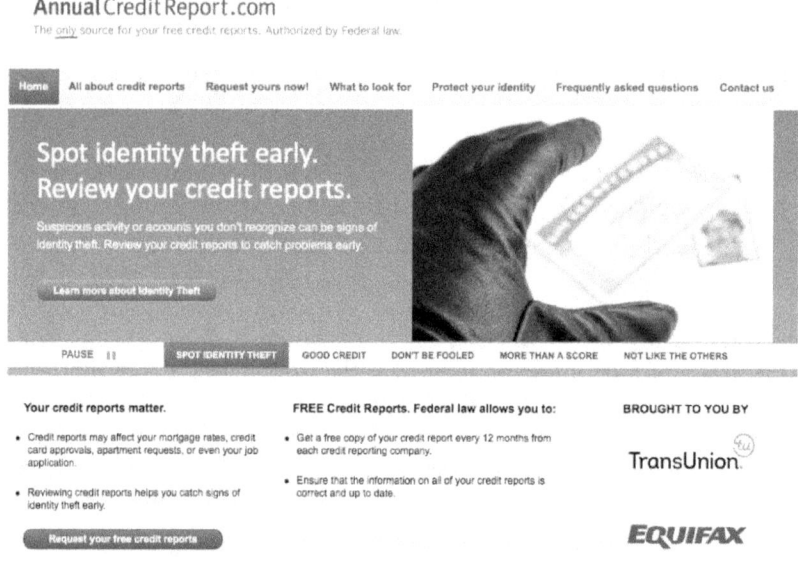

Nice interface and easy to use. Make sure to answer the questions correctly so you receive the credit reports.

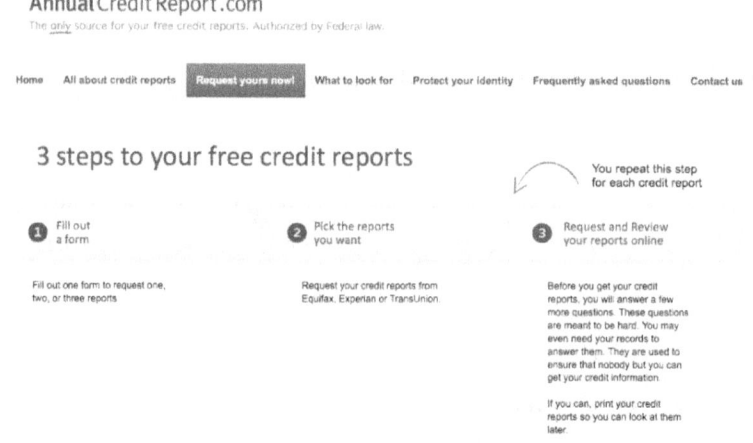

It provides a copy of all three credit agency (Equifax, Transunion, Experian) reports for FREE! Yes, see if nothing else I just saved you the cost of the book already. Many folks spend $20-30 just to get a copy of their credit reports without realizing you can do this for no cost. Once you have a copy of your credit reports, if you find any incorrect, wrong, false or negative information then DISPUTE IT right away! Get that crap and damaging junk off your life financial balance sheet immediately. It will hurt your chances of free money and financial golden success. As someone who had to repair my credit at one point, I learned this lesson the hard way. Fortunately time heals all wounds and with common sense you FICO score will look fantastic sooner than later. Keep reading as I offer some tips on how to legally fix your credit for FREE in the book.

Now, the next ingredient you will need is to get a recent copy of the local Pennysaver or junk mailing papers. Yes, for once the much hated and frequently discarded series of papers and mailers that end up in the trash can will be your new friend on saving each week to get free goodies! Trust me, as you will see later on in the journey, you will be glad to keep these on hand for your next happy meal. As they say, one man's trash is another man's treasure! This will ring so true soon for you.

Third- either a computer with internet or access to a computer with internet access. In order to take advantage of deals and check things quickly you will need a computer with internet. While this is not an issue these days with most people, those who are financially limited can use a local library with computers and internet for FREE! Yes, you don't need to run out and buy the most expensive computer and internet if you are short on cash. After all that is why you bought this book, right? To save money and get money back at no cost.

Since we have completed our shopping tour and assembled the required tools and ingredients then we can get started on that free money we all want to get back. And the most ironic thing you will learn is to love that much hated item from banks called the **CREDIT CARD!**

2 CREDIT CARD MAGIC

If you have completed the initial homework assignment earlier from the first chapter then you are ready to win big on one of the best free money tips that I have EVER discovered: the magic of credit card perks!

Yes, the much maligned, hated and scorned love and hate affair we have with banks and credit cards can be turned from pain and suffering to joy and financial power. All that it takes is a little self discipline and common sense. I will share my secrets that are little known and often ignored by the vast majority of people. The credit cards with perks, freebies and benefits. First let's talk turkey about the various kinds of credit cards.

I recommend the following websites that provide excellent overview of the different credit card types:

https://www.creditkarma.com/creditcards/

http://www.nerdwallet.com/blog/top-credit-cards/nerdwallets-best-cash-back-credit-cards/

You can search based on type of credit card as well as types available based on how good or bad your credit score is. Now you know why having good understanding of your credit is key before we get started.

Credit Karma is great for the wide variety of choices and research available to you at your fingertips.

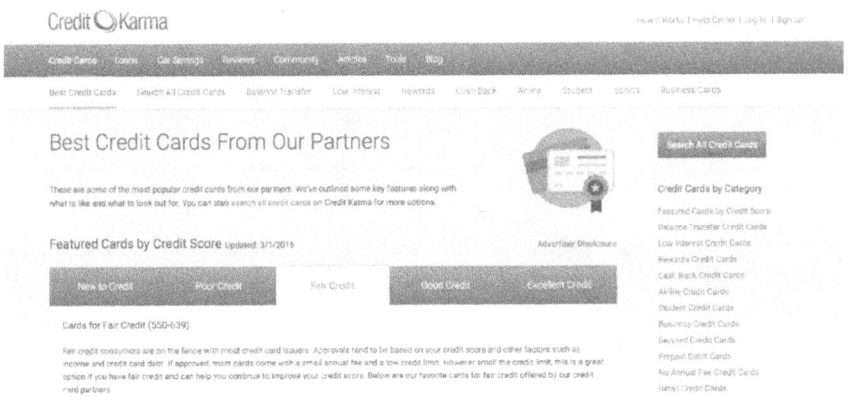

Nerd Wallet is similar but has a different user interface and method.

Personally, I much prefer Credit Karma as it has more features in researching different credit card types as well as the ability to save your favorite choices for later viewing. Another website that you will want to bookmark and save for later viewing is http://www.bankrate.com

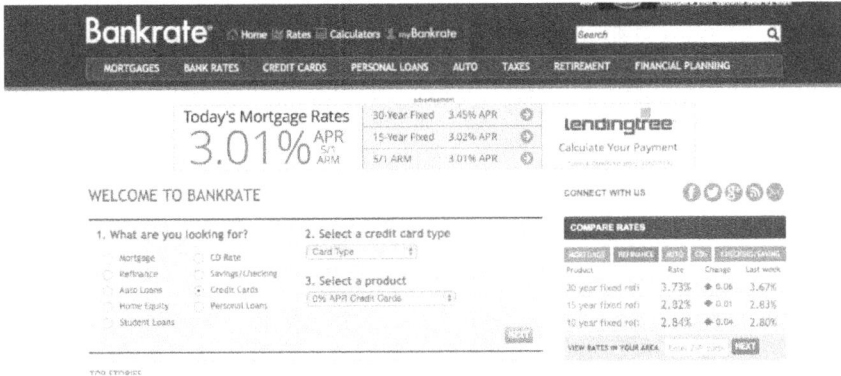

Bankrate is a great website for research in comparing credit rates and benefits. There are online free calculators and additional financial tools at your disposal as well. Now lets take a trip to the credit card buffet and look at some different types of credit cards that return free money and many other nice perks!

Credit Card Types

Like the grocery market or auto dealer lot, there are hundreds and hundreds of different credit card types for all budgets, credit backgrounds and purposes. I will guide you through the best ones based on what kind of free money perk you want to get.

Airline Travel Mileage Credit Cards

So do you like to take nice vacations to Europe, the Caribbean and Hawaii? Want to fly for free? Well the mileage airline credit cards are your new best friend! Save thousands on expensive airfare as well as get free complimentary upgrades to business and first class. Now I call that a steal!

Based on research from NerdWallet the best overall two travel airline mileage credit cards are the United Mileage Plus Explorer and Citi AAdvantage domestic airline mileage travel card.

Best for frequent domestic travelers (tie)

United MileagePlus® Explorer Card

★★½☆☆ (24 Reviews)

Apply Now 🔒

⊙ Show Details

Earn double miles on United ticket purchases, 1 mile per dollar spent on everything else. Start with 30,000 bonus miles after you spend $1,000 on purchases in the first 3 months from account opening. Free checked bag. Priority boarding. Bonus for adding an authorized user. 10,000-mile bonus each year you spend $25,000. Two annual one-time United Club passes. $0 intro annual fee for the first year, then $95.

Benefits of the United MileagePlus® Explorer Card:

- The sign-up bonus isn't the best, but the spending requirement to receive it is low.
- Chase offers a rewards bonus for adding an authorized user with several of its consumer cards, but you won't see this kind of bonus with most other airline cards.

QUICK WIN:

Choose the travel airline credit card based on the airline you use the most. For example, if you already are a frequent United Airline member then join that card program. On the other hand, if you fly Delta Airlines frequently then join and get the Delta preferred airline credit card. You want to rack up as many miles as quickly as possible on one airline instead of spreading your airline miles across too many different airlines and card programs.

If you are a globe trotter across the planet and want freebies to fly international the best airline credit card program might be the **British Airways Visa Signature Card** as shown below.

Best for frequent international travelers

 **British Airways Visa Signature* Card**

★ ★ ½ ☆ ☆ (4 Reviews)

Apply Now 🔒

on Chase's secure website

🔽 Show Details

Earn 3 Avios on every $1 spent on British Airways purchases, 1 Avios per dollar spent on everything else. Get 50,000 bonus Avios after you make $2,000 in purchases within the first 3 months of account opening. Get a Travel Together ticket each year you spend $30,000 or more on your card. No foreign transaction fees. $95 annual fee.

Benefits of the British Airways Visa Signature* Card:

- The British Airways Visa Signature* Card has a high sign-up bonus, with a comparatively low spending requirement to get it.
- With no foreign transaction fees, the British Airways Visa Signature* Card is an ideal card for international travel.
- Those who spend more than $30,000 a year can use their Travel Together ticket to bring a companion on a flight

For myself, as I plan more international trips abroad, I plan to get the international card to save on expensive flights to overseas locations. Plus you save on the nasty expensive foreign transaction fees as well. That can add up to serious savings on a trip. For example, if you withdraw money from a foreign bank ATM or buy dinner at a restaurant in Paris, you can save hundreds in these fees!

There are dozens of airline mileage credit card programs so you can read them on Nerdwallet and Credit Karma for the best one to meet your needs. Now let's talk about the next way to save money on travel and that is hotel credit cards!

Hotel Points Credit Cards

Probably one of the most expensive costs of a vacation or trip is the hotel stay. With hotels averaging over $100 per night in the United States and often triple the cost abroad especially in western Europe, this cost adds up quickly. Now wouldn't it be great to save thousands of dollars on a nice trip? When I was in Buenos Aires recently on a vacation, I used my hotel credit card points to save over a thousand dollars on my trip! Plus the previous airline credit card points paid for my international business class flight so I ended up with essentially a free vacation trip to one of the most glamorous places in the entire world. Let's take a glimpse into a few of these hotel benefit cards to see what they offer.

Best for frequent hotel guests

Starwood Preferred Guest®
Credit Card from American
Express

✩ ✩ ✩ ✩　　(13 Reviews)

Apply Now 🔒

on American Express's secure
website

⊙ Show Details

Earn up to 5 points on every $1 spent at Starwood hotels and resorts, 1 point on every dollar spent elsewhere. Get 35,000 bonus Starpoints® after you use your new Card to make $3,000 in purchases within the first 3 months. Transfer points to dozens of frequent flier programs, typically at a rate of 1:1. Annual fee: $0 for the first year, then $95.

Benefits of the Starwood Preferred Guest® Credit Card from American Express:

- You can turn your SPG hotel spending into free flights by transferring your points to more than two dozen frequent flier programs.

Starwood hotels are some of the nicest and most luxurious properties on the planet. Why not get free travel and stay in a plush hotel on your next business trip or vacation? While some of these hotel card programs do charge an annual fee, if you use the credit card enough the cost more than pays for itself many times over. Think about it: if you spend $100 once a year for the card and save a **thousand bucks** on that next trip then it more than pays for itself many times over.

QUICK WIN

Find programs that charge either no annual fee or provide a free one year credit card membership to save big.

Special Perk Credit Cards

These beauties let you save on a wide variety of goods and services from electronics to groceries to new cars!
One example is the Lexus Credit and BMW credit card. For example, if you own a Lexus or other car, you can save big on auto maintenance and purchase programs.

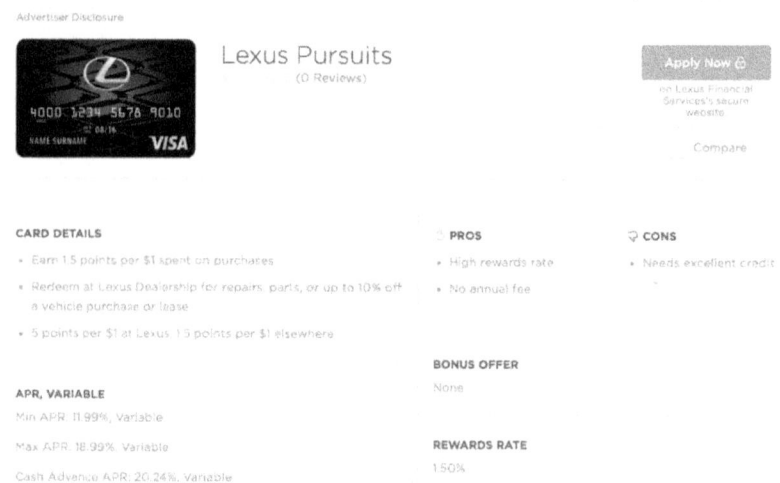

Of course there are dozens of similar auto credit card types. Check out NerdWallet and Credit Karma for additional details or use Google to search different brands. As a Mercedes-Benz fan of high performance AMG cars, one credit card worthy of consideration is the AMEX Mercedes card.

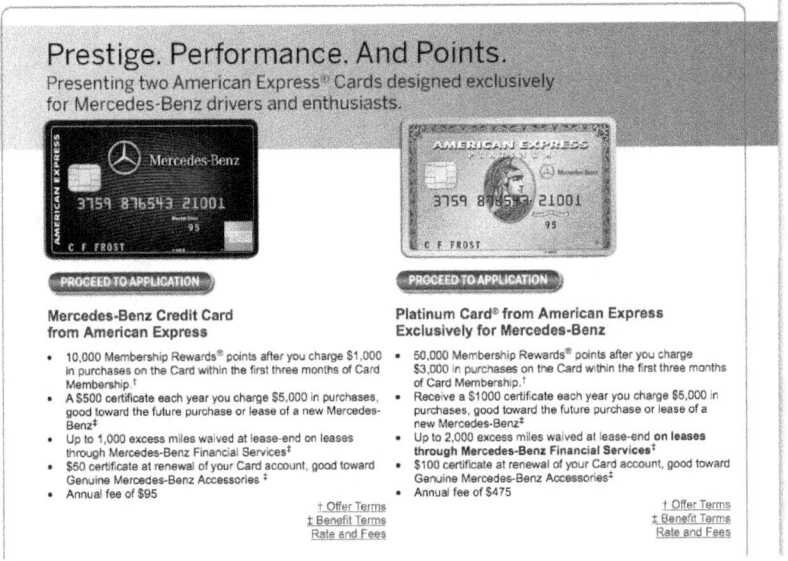

Details available on the AMEX site

https://www262.americanexpress.com/apply-card/personal-card/012/16580

So these are great if you plan to eventually buy a new or used car and want to save tons of cash on auto needs. Now lets take a look at another cool useful money back credit card type. If you are an audiophile or home theater freak and love gaming, the Sony Credit card from Capitol One Bank just may very well be worth consideration.

SonyCard

Earn points toward entertainment and more, plus

Get a $50 credit

after your first purchase**

Apply Now NO ANNUAL FEE

SonyCard

4000 1234 5678 9010

12/12 TO/18
LEE X CARDHOLDER **VISA**

NO ANNUAL FEE

Earn points toward Sony® products with every Sony Card℠ purchase

The Sony Card from Capital One® is the card that lets you earn points toward your favorite electronics, entertainment, once-in-a-lifetime experiences and more... *with no annual fee.*

- 5X POINTS on Sony purchases at authorized retailers with purchase confirmation†
- 3X POINTS on music and video downloads, movie theaters and rentals, and digital streaming and subscription services††
- 1X POINTS on all other purchases

Plus, save on interest with a 0% intro APR on purchases until December 2016! After that, a variable APR between 14.24% - 24.99% applies.*

Get a $50 statement credit

Apply now and, once approved, you'll get a $50 credit on your Sony Card statement after your first purchase. Now is a great time to get the Sony Card.

Apply Now NO ANNUAL FEE

0% intro APR on purchases

See how fast your Sony Rewards points can add up!

PURCHASES	AMOUNT	POINTS MULTIPLIER	POINTS EARNED
Sony Flat Screen TV	$2,000	5X	10,000
Amazon Prime Membership	$99	3X	297
Family Night at the Movies (2 times)	$96	3X	288
Groceries	$450	1X	450

TOTAL POINTS you could earn in just one month: **11,035 POINTS**

Actual amount of points you earn will depend on your credit limit and purchase activity.

One attractive feature of the SonyCard is no annual fee and a nice 0% intro APR to save on purchases. So if you plan to eventually buy a TV and other electronics, why not earn points and have the credit to get a new Sony Playstation 4 for free? Sounds like a deal to me!

Now keep in mind we have barely scratched the surface on the thousands of types of credit card programs that exist and there are department store and gas station credit cards as well. However, based on market research and personal experience, these really don't add the same level of value and cash back that the cash back, travel and airline credit card programs provide to you as a consumer. I have saved the best for last the cash back credit card! Let us move and see how to really win big on free money back.

Cash Back Credit Cards- My Personal Favorite!

Now of all the perks, who doesn't like cold hard cash that you can get for FREE and use any way that you choose? Well I certainly do! Best of all you don't have to rob a bank and you don't have to participate in a slimy multi-level marketing (MLM) pyramid scheme program. It is all one hundred per cent legal, proven and best of all free! In life we know that most things that sound too good to be true are exactly that and that life does not offer such thing as a free lunch. However, cash back credit cards are the one gift that banks have been generous to consumers and little known as well by most people. There are different types of cash back credit cards and my two personal favorites are the Bank of America Cash Back credit card and the US Bank Cash Back credit card.

Proven Results

Last year, I performed an experiment on two of the many cash back credit card programs to see how well they performed. The first was US Bank Cash back Credit Card. Some details on the US Bank Cash Back Credit card program below. You can find these at

https://www.usbank.com/splash/credit-cards/cash-plus/sem/index.html?&kw=%22usbankcashcard%22

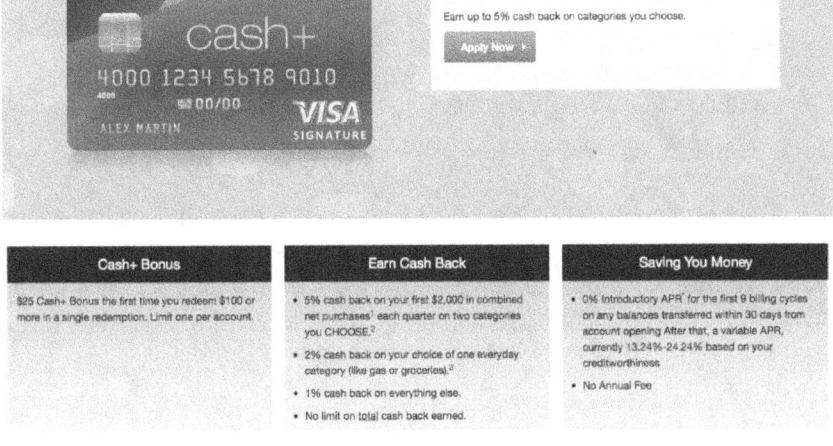

13

One things I really love about the US Bank Cash+ Visa credit card is that you earn 5% cash back right away and then 1-2% cash back on anything you want. Plus there is no limit on how much cash back you can receive. Second, there is no annual fee costs like many perk cards such as AMEX charge you. As a real testimonial and experience, I have great personal success on this cash back card and now you can as well.

Here is an example of how much free cash you can get in a short period of time.

Below is the cash back FREE I received from US Bank credit card last year:

U.S. Bank Cash+ Visa Signature® Card ·

Rewards History

Current Rewards Balance	$54.85
Rewards Available for Redemption	$54.85

Rewards Details

Rewards Earned (Program to Date)	$216.63
Rewards Redeemed (Program to Date)	$161.78
Rewards Balance (Program to Date)	$54.85
Bonus Rewards Since Last Statement	$0.00
Adjustments Since Last Statement	$0.00
Package Bonus Rewards	$0.00

This is from less than a year of using the credit card too!

The other cash back credit card that I highly recommend is the Bank of America Cash Back card. It provides a no nonsense high rate of cash back and no annual fee. You can apply and get this awesome cash back credit card at https://www.bankofamerica.com/credit-cards/products/cash-back-credit-card.go or visit a local Bank of America branch for details.

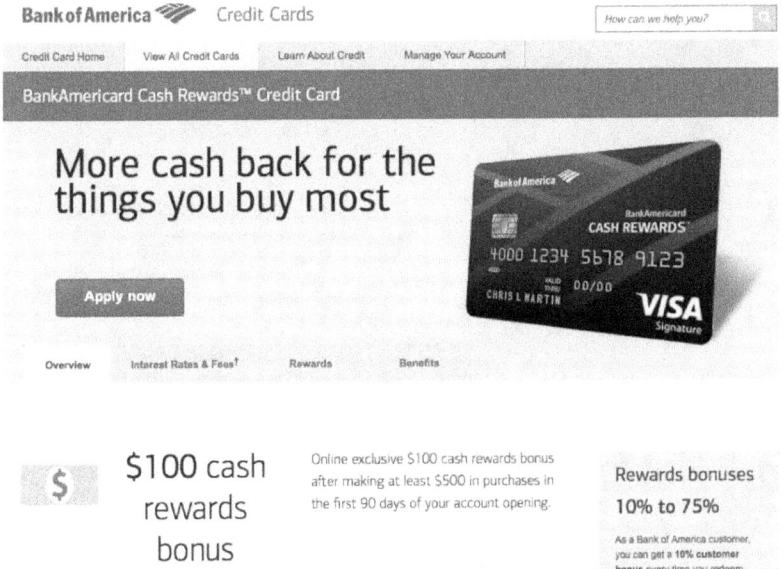

What I really love about this cash back credit card is the high rate of return for cash back on everyday purchases like groceries, gas and food and dining out at restaurants and cafes. Plus they have a higher rate of cash back on these daily needs that you are going to have to buy anyways.

Earn cash back everywhere, every time

1% cash back on every purchase
2% cash back at grocery stores
3% cash back on gas
Grocery store/gas bonus rewards on up to $1,500 grocery/gas quarterly spend.

 No annual fee†

Enjoy no annual fee while earning more cash back for the things you buy most.

 **Introductory rate for 12 billing cycles**

Applies to purchases and to any balance transfers made within 60 days of opening your account.

For me the best results on daily basis have been this credit card. It racks up the free money back very quickly!

Now for my other cash back card from Bank America, the results over a year are even more lucrative! Here is a brief example of recent cash back for FREE with the Bank America credit card that I was able to accomplish with no effort.

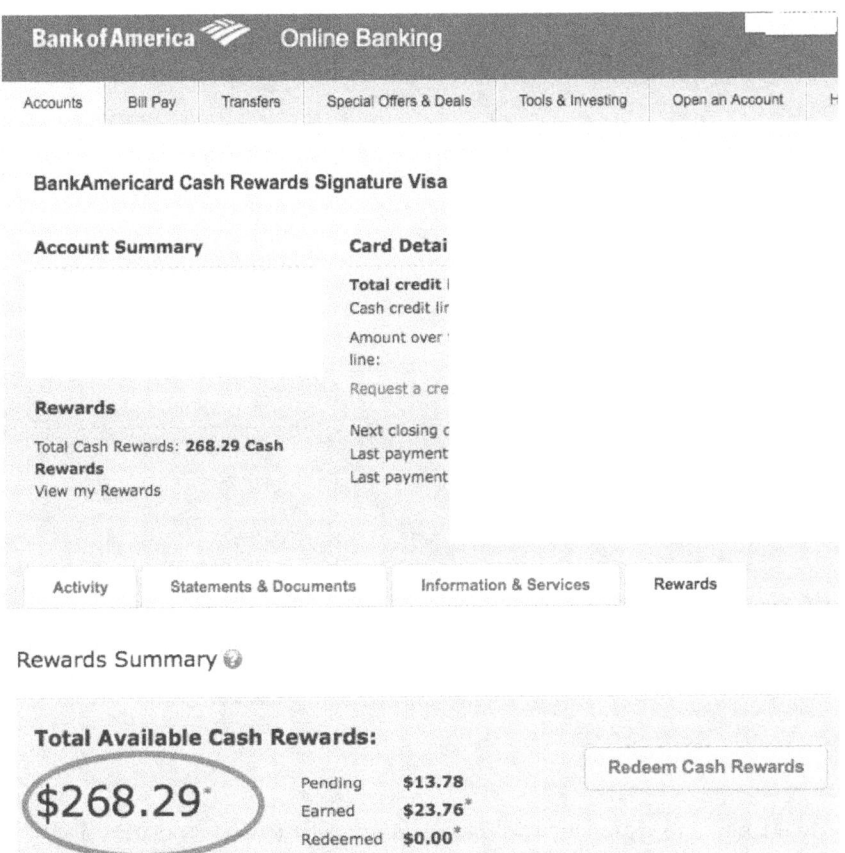

As you can see the results are amazing! Tons of free cash for no cost doing everyday activities! We cover some strategies later on how to best maximize your free cash results. When I ran the beta test last year for my new Bank of America cash back credit card, **I earned over a thousand dollars** in FREE MONEY back! Now you can do the same and enjoy the free cash back to spend anyway your little heart desires.

Free Points and Trips- Honorable Mention

Now we come to the runner up category of perk based credit cards the ones that mix and match points for hotel and airline travel as well as rebates toward consumer goods. The two winners in this category are the Chase

Sapphire Preferred (http://www.chase.com) and the Blue Cash Preferred Card from American Express (http://www.amex.com) .

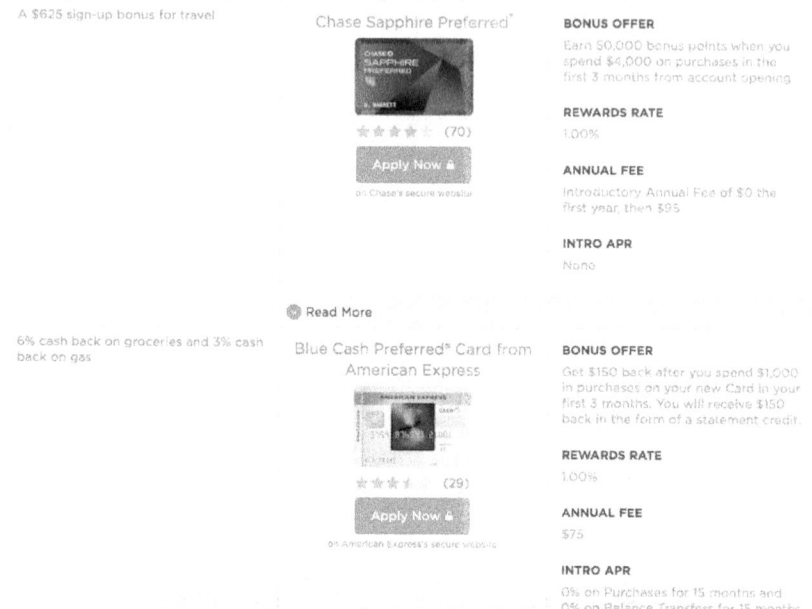

While I have no experience or these cards the reviews are positive and win spots on Credit Karma and NerdWallet lists for best overall credit cards. Since the focus here is free money back, these are supplemental cards as an option for a serious business traveler.

Well I hope you enjoyed this chapter. It offers you plenty of free money available if you obtain one of these money saving credit cards. We recommend that you pay off each card monthly in full to avoid charges and maximize free cash back. I offer some good solid tips later on in the book how to do these things.

3 BANKING VOODOO!

The last chapter showed you how to double and triple your money back if you follow the instructions. Now to one of my favorite free money secrets: bank accounts! One relatively unknown free money tip is to open a new bank account at no cost other than basic minimum amount to receive the free money perks from the bank. I learned about these programs via coupons in the mail that I almost discarded. After walking into Chase Bank with coupon in hand, the friendly bank teller helped me open a new account and deposited the free cash into it as well! He was surprised that most people ignore these free cash deals and throw away the special offers! I told him that someday I would write a book showing people how to get free money back and he smiled.

Get Free Money to Open New Bank Account

Coupons that are often discarded by the masses promise free money to open a savings account at low cost.

One little known tip is that many banks offer a promo to open a new savings or checking account. That is they give you free money!

Several large banks provide such free money!

US Bank provides the START program which gives you up to $100 in free MONEY! Yes, believe it or not, FREE MONEY!

https://www.usbank.com/bank-accounts/savings-accounts/start-smart-savings-program.aspx?ecid=PS_15299&mkwid=sG1rq3tQp%7Cpcrid%7C76775080731%7Cpkw%7Copening%20savings%20account%7Cpmt%7Cp%7Cpdv%7Cc&sdsmid=G1rq3tQp

To show the free money offer the below US Bank explains in summary what freebies you receive:

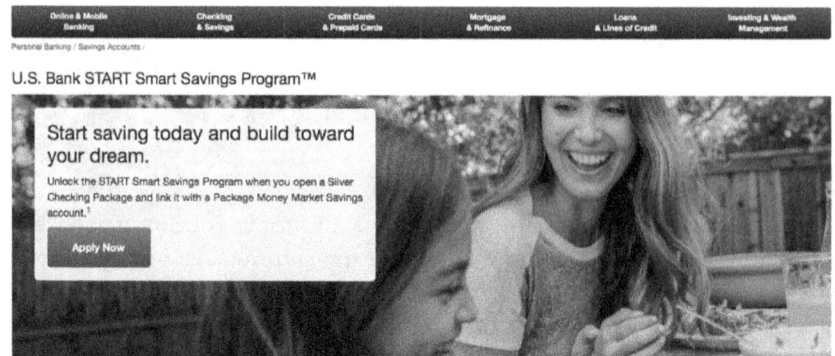

As a US Bank customer and proof that I used this program, getting $100 free money back was quite satisfying! The reason I wrote this book is that I wanted to share these insider secrets with you all so that you can enjoy the same rewards that I enjoy risk free.

Now the ultimate free money back program that I have personally used is with Chase Bank. They provide serious free money back when you open a new bank account. All that you need to do is either visit a local Chase Bank branch or visit the following website to get the coupon for free money:

https://coupon.chaseoffers.com/banking/prep.do?ID=41514&jp_cmp=rb
/378413/aff/3_4/na&CODE=.XA.lMdSsKg-
5yHPycbMB4k7v3.Ku._Wkw&MSC=.XA.lMdSsKg-
5yHPycbMB4k7v3.Ku._Wkw

CHASE ◆

Get up to **$250**

with a new Chase checking and savings account

Send me bonus coupon

Enter Email Address

*By entering your e-mail address here, we will only use it to send the coupon and it will not be used for other promotions or shared with third parties.

Enjoy up to $**250** on us

Get $150

As a new Chase checking customer, when you open a **Chase Total Checking®** account¹ and set up direct deposit²

OR

Get $100

When you open a new **Chase Savings℠** account¹ and deposit $10,000 or more in new money within 10 business days, and maintain a $10,000 balance for 90 days²

Another route to Chase free money back is to use the direct link below:

https://www.chase.com/checking/offer/get-coupon-bandujo-combo-1.html?&mkwid=EYOUhrZ6_dc&pcrid=106740671051&jp_cmp=rb%2FTier+1+-+Brand+-+MBM%2Fsea%2Fna%2Fchase+coupons_Phase2_Tier+1

For my acid test as part of research for this book, I actually really opened accounts with both US Bank and Chase to see how the benefits worked. Chase was the best one and dumped $150 cash into my new Chase account. US Bank gave me the $50 free money card when I opened the account. So right away at no risk, I received $200 in free money! Not bad for little to no real work, huh? Now you can do the same! For me, nothing beats free money for no real work other than to follow the low hanging opportunities that most people ignore and overlook.

QUICK TIP

One caveat: you will need to leave a small amount of cash in the new bank account over a period of time usually from six months to a year to earn the free money offer that the bank provides. The reason why banks do this for consumers is to allow them to float large amounts of money on credit to loan to other people. By doing so, the bank is thankful and kicks you down with free money! They actually don't make money on this. So now you are wondering how the heck can banks give away all this free money? Easy! They loan shark credit at brutal rates like 5-20% to other consumers who want to buy cars, homes and so forth.

Now that we have covered two amazing free cash back strategies, let us move on to the third overlook strategy of coupons that most people trash these days instead of using to earn free goodies.

4 COUPON POWER!

When I was poor kid, I used to help my mother cut out coupons from the weekly flyers to use for buying groceries. We were dirt poor but learned to survive on coupons. This taught me a valuable lesson in financial matters. I love coupons and flyers. Chock full of goodies for all things that appeal to everyone you can save hundreds and thousands of dollars each year. I love the restaurant specials and free offers too.

Today I received a free coupon in the mail from one of my favorite local chain fast food restaurants, Chipotle.

With no obligation to buy anything, you can enjoy a nice meal for free! Anyways, most folks throw away and ignore these valuable money saving coupons. The trick is to separate the wheat from the chaff. Often the golden nuggets of free meals and drink specials are mixed in with the traditional supermarket grocery store ads and coupons. Now, don't get me wrong, I like saving on fruits, vegetables, and meat as well. However, I much prefer a free meal!

Now that we live in the digital and social media age, you can even get these money saving and cash back deals at your fingertips anywhere you go on your ipad, Android or iphone in seconds.

Groupon (www.groupon.com) , Living Social (www.livingsocial.com) are two popular website programs that are great to use for saving money an any fun meal or event.

Groupon

Lets take a look at why I love Groupon and why you should too as well if you don't already!

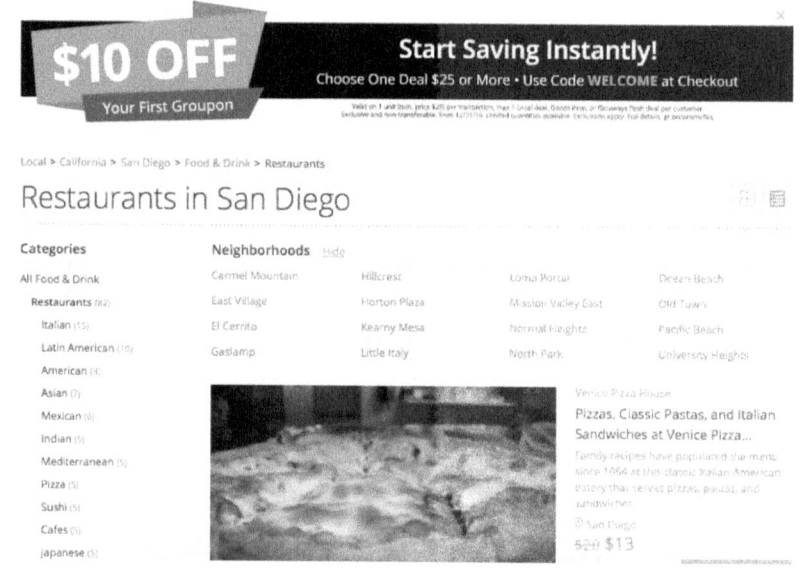

Do you like to eat? Well, I sure do! That's why I go to the gym as eating good food is not cheap. Groupon has amazing discounts for food and more. If you want to have an adventure you can do that as well! Want a manicure or car wash at low price? Why Groupon can help you based on where you live or currently are hanging out at.

Living Social

At http://www.livingsocial.com you can enjoy incredible savings on good times.

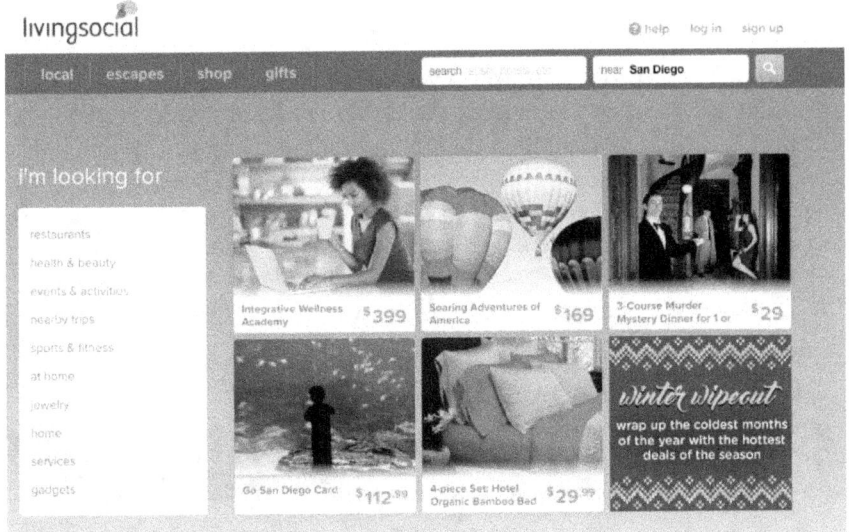

For adventures and thrill seekers, the Living Social site has discounts and freebies on fun times. I love the focus on local and national deals for everything fun under the sun and then some.

Like Groupon, Living Social has discounts on food and dining and also recreational pursuits. Both Living Social and Groupon are free to join to save right away on fun times and everything you can think of.

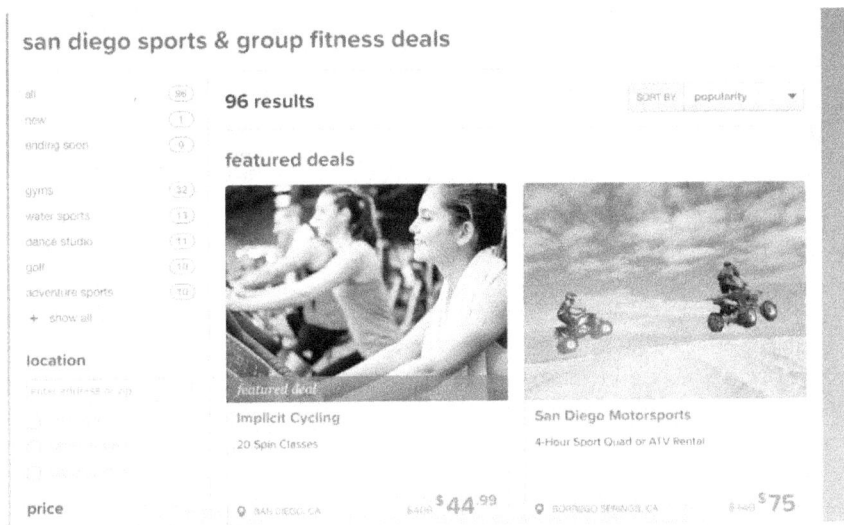

So of course you probably throw away coupons but with the online tools you no longer need to worry if you visit these two sites. I do recommend keeping the flyers for deals as well. On a side note, I am sad to report that the infamous Pennysaver company that used to send weekly flyers out when I was a kid is no longer going to be around. Here is the story in case you are interested in reading it later online:

http://www.sandiegouniontribune.com/news/2015/may/26/pennysaver-closure-layoffs-publishing-media-ads/

I read from last year in the San Diego newspaper that circulates in my home town that due to lack of cash and revenues, the long time Pennysaver is going bye bye. Like the closing of Borders Bookstores and many other large institutions, they failed to pay attention to the digital online revolution. So sad. Anyways there are two other companies that distribute real print coupons- MoneyMailer and ValPak. I get these every week and save tons in deals. Now you can as well.

5 PROMO WIZARDRY

Promos are the best bang for free stuff and low hanging fruit waiting to be picked for the taking.

Happy Hour Specials

As a beer and food lover, I always scope out the best watering spots for happy hour deals. The trick is to be able to find the times and days when the half off meals and drink specials are in effect. One trick is to use websites online like Yelp! (http://www.yelp.com) for reviews and insights. My favorite new Happy Hour place in Ocean Beach, California near San Diego is Ragland Public house and they have great half off deals on pints and food.

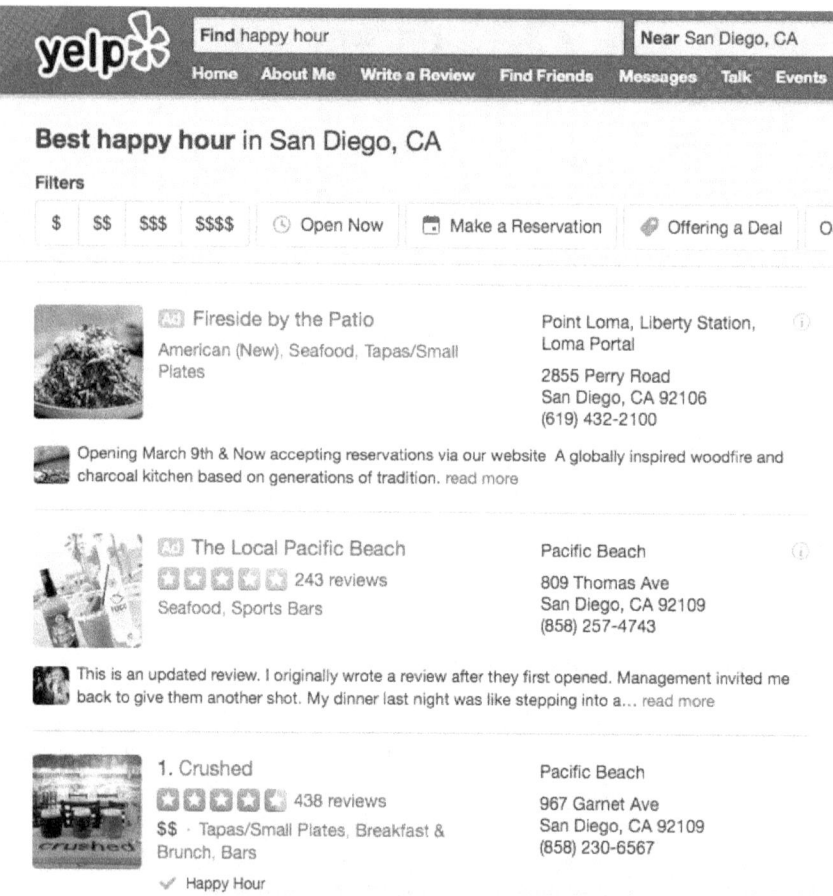

The great thing about Yelp is that you can search on location and type of establishment. Reviews are candid and offer real feedback on the happy hour deals and food and service. Now what can beat a good happy hour deal? Yup, you guessed it my friends, a free meal at a top dining establishment!

Free meals

These come in mail flyers more often than not and usually sadly end up neglected and in the garbage can by most people who receive these in the mail.

QUICK TIP:

Check and read your daily and weekly mail carefully and do not blindly throw stuff away!

Birthday Magic

One little trick that I love using every year comes on my birthday. Many restaurants and cafes offer a free meal discount, appetizer, coffee drink and more! I recommend scoping out your favorite places to eat and drink coffee to get the heads up on the freebies on your birthday!

You can search on Google under free birthday meals like I did for San Diego.

http://sandiegan.com/free-birthday-meals-san-diego/

That is one website that has the scope for my local area.
Usually chain restaurants like Applebees and Starbucks provide the same birthday special free offer in most cities and states.

One other tip is to sign up for online restaurant clubs to get deals, coupons and special offers. These are free no cost and only take seconds to enroll online. You can even do it while on the go with your ipad or iphone. One example is Black Angus has a free steak dinner on your birthday!

So if you visit the Black Angus website and enroll in the club free program then on your next birthday you can enjoy a free steak dinner! How awesome that would be to treat yourself on your special day? I love steak and this is a great free offer. Here is the link:

http://blackangus.fbmta.com/members/UpdateProfile.aspx?Action=Subscribe&_Theme=23622320277&InputSource=W

Starbucks has a free reward program that gives you a free coffee drink of your choice when you sign up online. Details are available at https://www.starbucks.com/card/rewards

Here is the information on the different perks including the free Starbucks coffee drink just for signing up online!

Welcome level

To earn your first rewards, just register a Starbucks, Teavana or La Boulange Card.

- Birthday drink or treat on us
- Birthday coupon for 15% off a purchase at Starbucks Store online
- Custom offers via email (be sure to opt in)

Green level

Collect five Stars within 12 months and you'll be in the Green level.

- Birthday drink or treat on us
- Birthday coupon for 15% off a purchase at Starbucks Store online
- Custom offers via email (be sure to opt in)
- **Free in-store refills on hot or iced brewed coffee and tea**

Gold level

Collect 30 Stars within 12 months and you're at the Gold level.

- Birthday drink or treat on us
- Birthday coupon for 15% off a purchase at Starbucks Store online
- Custom offers via email (be sure to opt in)

So that saves you anywhere from $2-5 on that expensive latte or mocha that you love to drink.

Never Dine Alone

Who says that two is company when three is a crowd? Well not when it comes to dining at fine restaurants and sharing the savings! Like the Chinese restaurant that offers more choices and dishes for the dinner special, the benefits add up quickly when you bring a friend, date or companion out to eat with you. Some great specials are in store when you have someone to share them with. Let's review a few good ones.

Buy One get One free

This is probably the oldest and most common special coupon in existence. You get these all the time in the mail for new restaurants and most people trash them. Groupon, Angie's List, and Living Social are famous for tons of these specials. However, one website is nice that shows these as the prime focus:

http://www.get1free.com

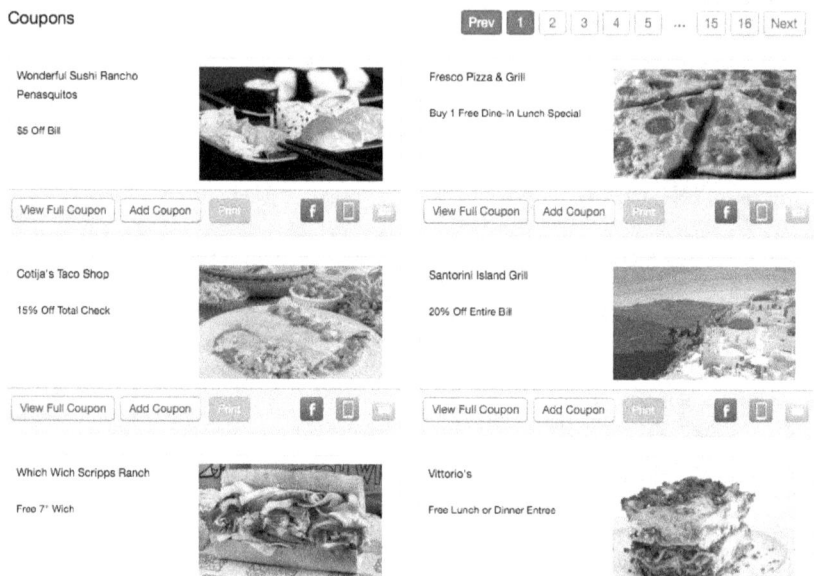

Here we have many buy one get one free meal deals. Google and weekly mailers showcase tons of these deals which is why I recommend reading the junk mail to find these hidden treasures. They make great date ideas to splurge on fantastic dinner dates without breaking the piggy bank!

Other specials are at chain restaurants for half off deals and buy one get one free as well. I love pizza and one of my favorite spots is called Pielogy (www.pielogy.com) and they have some of the best deals around if you sign up for the free online membership.

Free Haircuts and Odditiies

I even get free haircut coupons in the mail. Folks, haircuts are no longer cheap for the most part. When was the last time you were at Supercuts and paid $20 for a basic haircut? Well local salons want new business so they can give you a free haircut as part of welcome package to earn your business. I was able to get not one but THREE FREE haircuts last year this way! Saved me $60 quickly too.

6 FINANCIAL HORSE SENSE

Here we come to solutions to using and building good financial habits and instincts. This inner sense will make you wealthy over time and free of most financial worries and headaches.

WARNING!

It takes a wee bit of self discipline and delayed gratification to reach your goals of financial independence!

Now then we want to break things down for you in ten simple steps that make sense and can be followed by anyone from a first grader to a PhD scientist. The good news is that you don't need to have and MBA in Finance from Wharton or CPA in accounting to master these key steps to avoid financial ruin and disaster. In summary, I created a simple blue print of ten steps that will guide you to victory.

Ten Steps to Success
How to Develop Good Financial Common Sense

1. Create a budget
2. Write down expenses
3. Keep track of what you spend
4. Avoid Impulse buys and Emotional Spending
5. Buy only what you can afford right now
6. Pay all bills on time or early
7. Monitor credit and bank accounts religiously
8. Join a local investing club
9. Attend free financial seminars
10. Spend less and invest more

Create a Budget

Up until now you may have lived your life flying by the seat of your pants spending money with no real attention or though to where the dollars and cents wander off to each day, week, month and year. Then you wonder why you are always broke and in debt. Ok, I can empathize I have been there and know that its no fun or picnic. Also, I am not picking on you or slamming anyone. However, creating a simple budget of your cash on hand, current income and tracking what you spend will really accelerate your path to wealth. So let's start with a simple bare bones example.

We will use Susie Q and Johnny B Goode as our imaginary couple. Both earn together $1000 a week in combined income, live in San Diego, California and pay $1200 a month in rent and another $300 for gas, insurance and other expenses. Johnny is a nightclub promoter and DJ who loves spinning records in the hottest San Diego clubs and Susie Q is a hostess at an upscale Del Mar restaurant.

Susie Q and Johnny B Goode Budget

Income $48,000/annual - $1000/week- **$4000** month

After taxes estimated= $2680

Rent: $1200

Cell Phone: $200

Gas: $200

Total minimum monthly expenses: $1400

They have $1280 left monthly.

Well so what does our lovely young hip couple do after expenses? Yup, you guessed it! They love to go out and party with their other hipster coworkers and friends every weekend in the upscale Gaslamp district and in La Jolla and Del Mar clubs to be seen with other glam couples. They blow the money on $200 dinners, $100 concert tickets and $200 VIP bottle service bar tabs then wonder why they are in debt and broke all the time.

After meeting with a financial planner, they come up with revised budget after rent and expenses are paid to use the remaining **$1280**.

Groceries: $400/month

Movies: $100/month

Concert: $200/month

Night out on the town: $200

Total additional expenses: $900

That leaves them with $380 over to save and invest for a vacation and retirement! We recommend that they open a free bank account to get the $100-$200 bonus cash instead of blowing it on booze and junk. So even on a low salary in an expensive cost of living place like San Diego, California, it is possible to become financially independent and avoid credit and financial ruin! We also recommend they hire a tax professional to find new ways to save on taxes as well.

NOTE:

I am not a financial planner, CPA, nor an attorney, so this is **not** **intended** to provide any legal, accounting, or financial planning advice. For these areas, consult one of these specialists. In fact, I highly recommend consultation with a CPA and financial planner expert to help you structure your investments and maximize tax savings strategies with your finances! My CPA has paid for his services ten fold in tax savings and avoiding issues.

Create a Budget and Track it!

Now comes the grunt work that will provide rewards in spades the whole budget and expense tracking. Fortunately there are a wide variety of tools available for online expense and budget planning and tracking besides using old school paper and pencil methods. Many offer free trial periods then charge a small fee and others are free. Some good ones to consider:

Mint

https://www.mint.com

Mint provides a nice proven setup backed by Intuit of Quicken and Quickbooks fame.

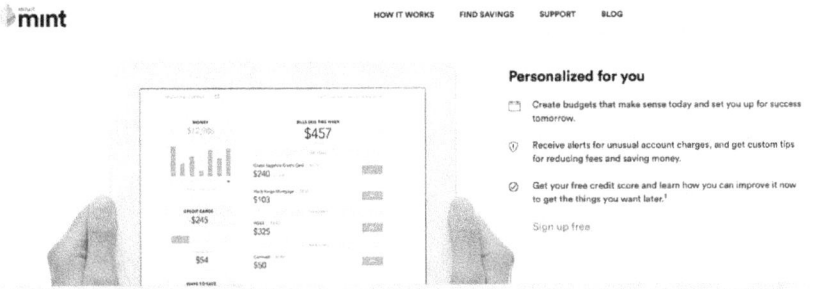

The beauty of Mint is that it provides tons of extra features like credit score reporting and financial budget integration tracking. The basic version is a free trial. For example, you can track your FICO credit score, expenses, bank account details and planning in one nice interface. Mint also offers free investment tips and options in case you want to invest extra income into IRA and different investment vehicles.

The only real downside of Mint based on my experience is that it is a resource hog! I had to close my applications on my Macbook to run it even though it is an online web program. So beware of that it takes a lot more horsepower to run than most applications. Then again, I am using a very old ten year old Macbook. However with that said, Mint is very powerful and feature rich and best of all, it is FREE! It won all kinds of PC Magazine awards for best online financial budget planning tools.

Here is an example budget I created with Mint.

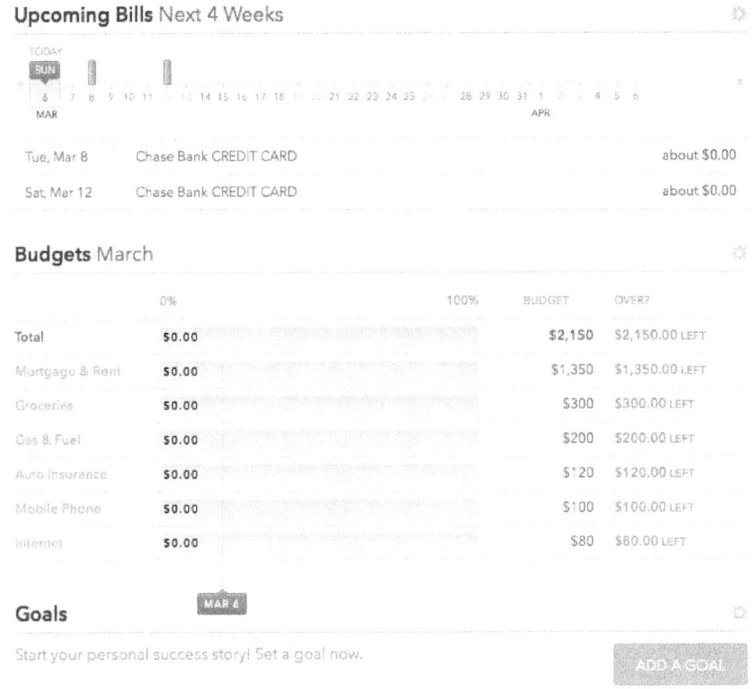

The trend analysis feature in Mint is worth mentioning as another nice to have feature for expense and budget planning.

Select a comparison ⬍

AUTO & TRANSPORT

Your Spending

CATEGORY	SPENDING
Auto & Transport	$256.23
Total	**$256.23**

Export to CSV

Most Purchases

1
on Auto & Transport

You can match up credit scores for free as well. They offer an extra monthly credit monitor service for a cost so ignore that as you really don't need to pay $16 a month for it! I love the overall dashboard from Mint that is lacking in the other budget online tools.

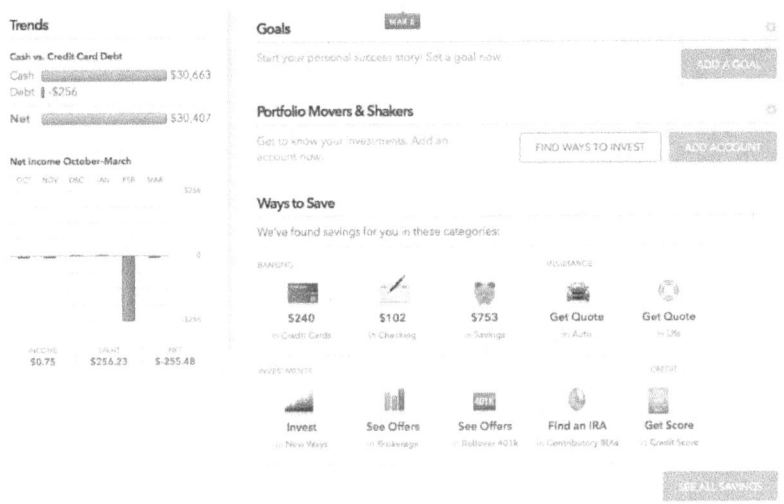

In my example budget dashboard here with Mint, I can track everything at my fingertips quickly and easily. I can also plan new goals to work toward financial success for a large purchase that I want to achieve in the future such as a new car or boat. The other tools are more basic and crude but get the job done. I recommend that you explore the different budget online tools to find what works best for your own situation.

Budget Simple

https://www.budgetsimple.com

Budget Simple offers a free version plus a cost version that offers a guarantee that it will save you money. Here is an overview of the application.

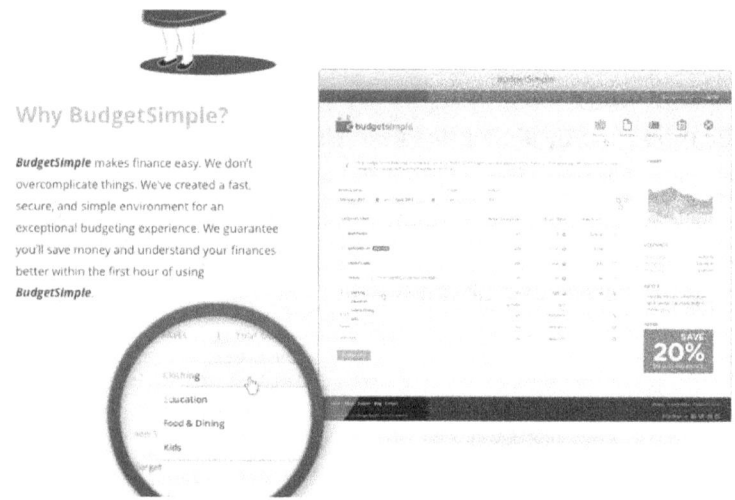

This is a fairly unknown budget online tool but it promises lots of cool new tips and features for online expense tracking and budgeting of household and personal expenses. Worth a look in my opinion. Free to sign up for basic version and nice menus walk you through the budget creation process. Below is my sample budget.

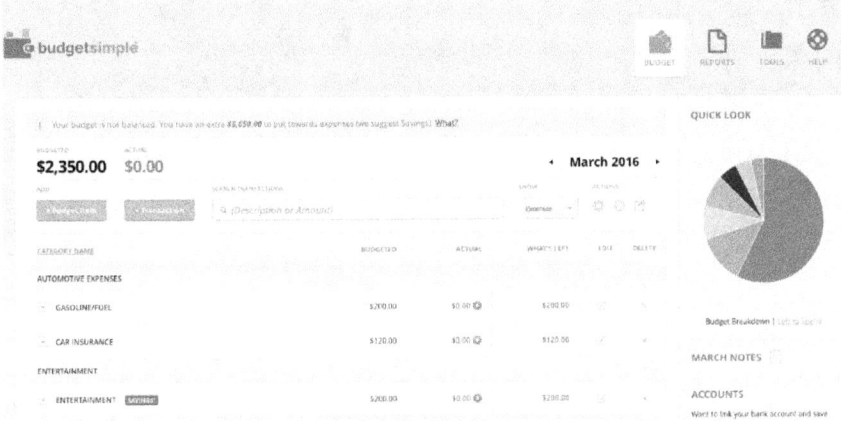

The nice thing about Budget Simple is the reports function lets you track expenses.

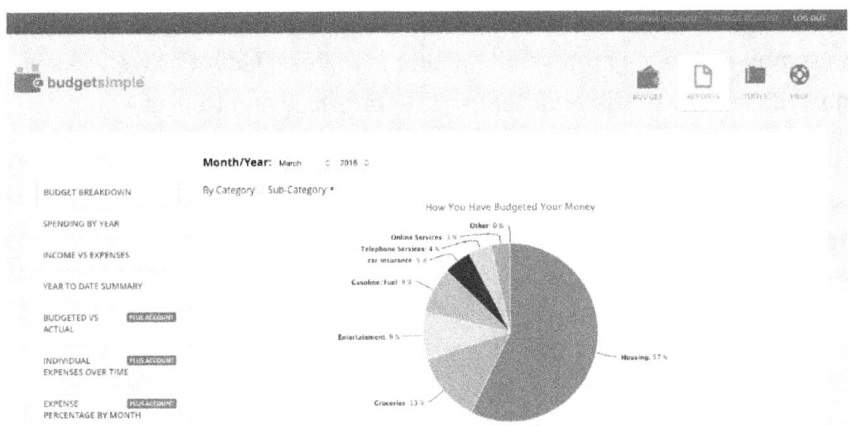

In my example budget report, I can view the pie chart to track where my money is being spent. It greatly simplifies the understanding over time where funds are sent and how to cut wasteful spending. Under tools, you can also plan how to pay off credit card debts over time.

Debt Payoff Tool

You can add your credit cards and other debts here. We'll show your progress in paying them off, and let you run projections to see how paying more will affect the time to be paid off (projections assume you make monthly payments, have no fees, and are not adding new debt).

If you've linked Credit Cards, we'll automatically add them here and keep the balances updated (regardless of whether you carry debt).

NAME	STARTING BALANCE	CURRENT BALANCE	MONTHLY PAYMENT	WILL BE PAID OFF	DELETE
			90.00		
Visa (15.99% APR)	4,500.00	$4,500.00 Update	Project Payoff	2023-01-06	

Projected Payoff

In summary, I much prefer Budget Simple to Pear Budget as we will see next. It is easier to use and cleaner user interface and free as well.

Pear Budget

https://pearbudget.com

Pear Budget is not as well known as Mint and offers a slightly different take on budget and expense tracking.

I tested it out and like the online interface for my example budget.

Planned Expenses for March

Monthly Expenses

CATEGORY	TO SPEND IN MARCH
cable	0.00
car gas	100.00
car insurance	120.00
car maintenance	200.00
cell phone	100.00
dining out	100.00
electric bill	35.00
groceries	400.00
haircuts	20.00
internet	80.00
medical	200.00
rent	1350.00
TOTAL	$2,705.00

Need to add a new category to your budget?

Irregular Expenses

CATEGORY	TO SET ASIDE IN MARCH	AVERAGE TO SET ASIDE TO MEET GOAL
clothing	50.00	50.00
entertainment	83.33	84.00
renter's insurance	16.66	17.00
TOTAL	$149.99	

Need to add a new category to your budget?

It lets you track well online anyplace via phone, ipad and computer.

While not as fancy as Mint, it is free and gets the job done without any fuss. For quick and dirty budget expense planning, it works fine however it lacks the nice features in Mint and Budget Simple. Now let's return to the grand daddy of them all, Microsoft Excel.

Microsoft Excel

This is what I have used for the past decade since I already have Microsoft Office and no need to buy it. Most folks have a computer with Microsoft Office these days and using Excel for basic stuff is pretty simple. I recommend that you create a simple formula to sum up monthly expenses automatically and another formula to subtract income from monthly expenses. For example:

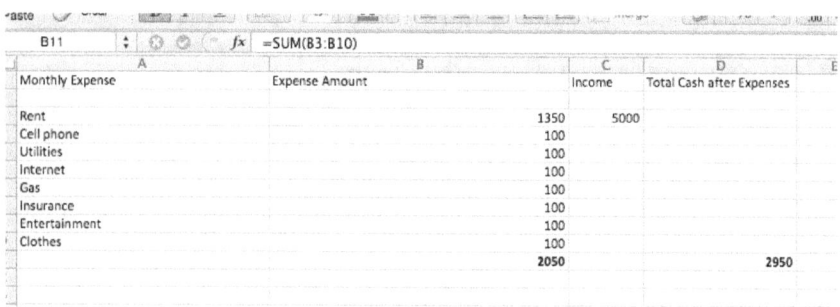

Then you can subtract expenses from income with a simple formula like this:

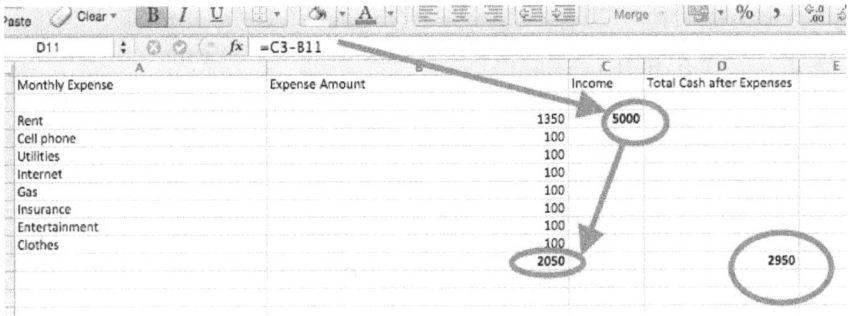

Entire books and online tutorials have been written and exist on using Excel so I refer you to Microsoft Excel website to learn how to manipulate the Excel formulas to suit your needs. Suffice it to say, I used a very simple formula to calculate my monthly budget in less than five minutes! While crude compared to the fancier online budget expense tracking tools, most people who own a computer already have Excel and no need to spend additional money to create a budget and track expenses.

Overall, the best of the bunch when it comes to integration and features is Mint from Intuit hands down winner. It links financial bank accounts and credit cards as well as investments into one nice slick online web user interface and has a portfolio of financial planning tools that blow away the other budget planner tools. For quick and dirty budget and expense planning, Microsoft Excel is the way to go if you have Office and spreadsheet experience. Try these and find what works out best for your own personal needs.

7 GOOD CREDIT

In this chapter I offer my insights to building, establishing and maintaining good credit. As a quick summary and tip sheet that you can keep in memory and for reference, the following ten tips will bring you to the good credit road that you will deserve for all the hard work.

My Ten Step Program to Flawless Credit

1. Track Credit Reports frequently

2. Dispute incorrect and negative information

3. Avoid too many inquiries on credit report

4. Do not apply for too many credit cards at one time

5. Utilize less than 30% of credit card limit

6. Pay credit cards in full every month

7. Spend less than you earn!

8. Save money in bank savings account and other investments.

9. Join a local credit union

10. Find lowest credit card rates and benefits

Credit Report Tracking

Often your credit report will have incorrect, outdated or just plain wrong negative information that unknown to you is hurting you in many ways besides pure finances. For example, if you apply for a high paying job, the potential employer will often check your credit report. If you have a history of delinquent credit, you may lose the opportunity to land the lucrative job.

Earlier, you pulled your free credit reports as part of the initial preparation exercise toward free money. Now, take a closer look for errors. If you do in fact find incorrect and negative information, you will need to dispute it with all three credit reporting agencies (CRA) to remove the black marks and errors from your reports. If verified and indeed you do owe past due accounts that went into collection to debt collection agencies, you will need to negotiate a deal with the collection agencies to have the bad mark removed. Now, let's take a closer look how to do this online to quickly expedite the process.

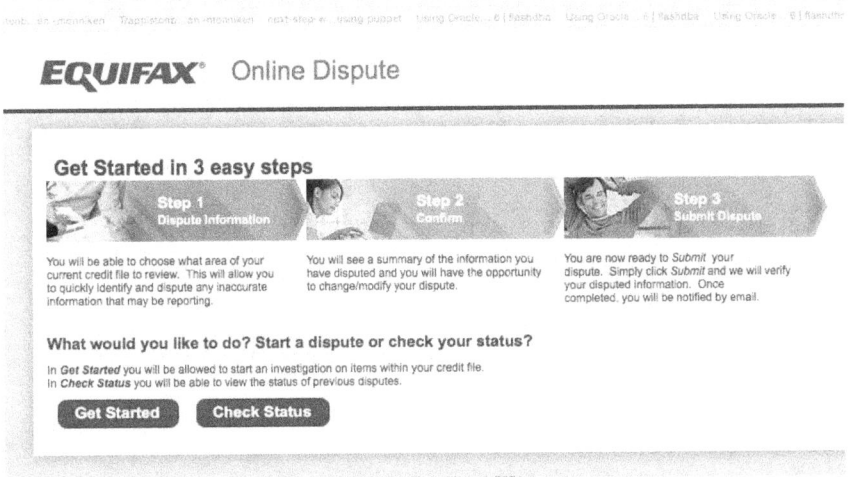

We will use Equifax as the example of how to dispute inaccurate credit report information. The other two credit reporting agencies, Experian and Transunion have similar online dispute forms.

After logging into Equifax website, it will ask you to answer a questionnaire and complete personal information on your address and date of birth.

Once you logon to Equifax website you will see the following options.

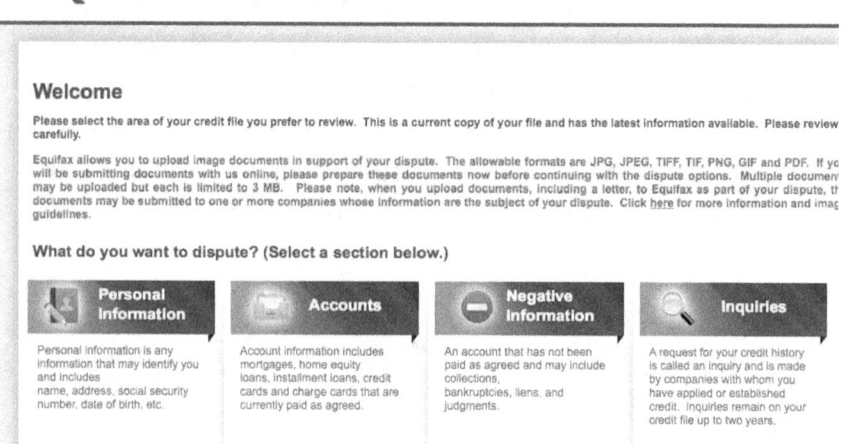

Choose each area to verify the correct and incorrect information. Since my credit is excellent and I have no bad marks, I want to dispute inquiries that can lower my credit score. The process for dispute on inaccurate personal information and negative information works the same way.

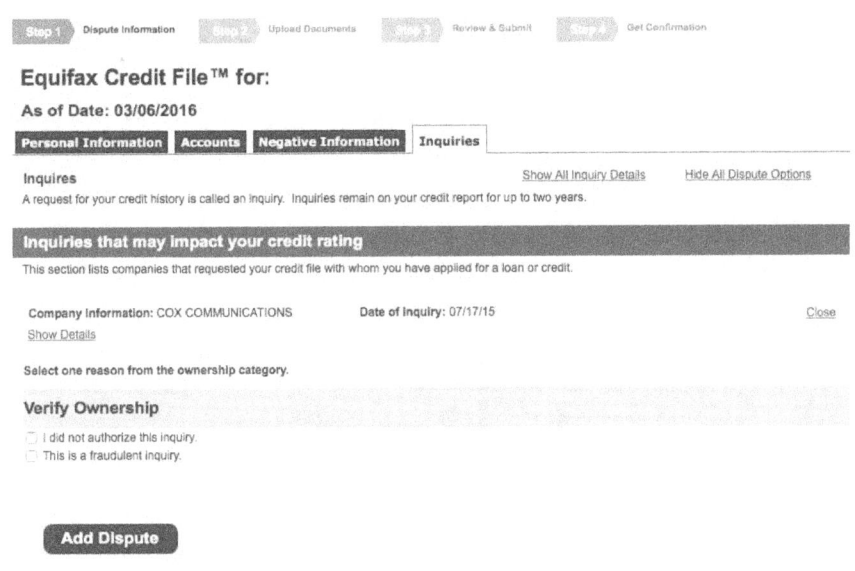

Check the box and add dispute.

Click on the submit button to process the online credit dispute. The online dispute form will show the item in process for dispute.

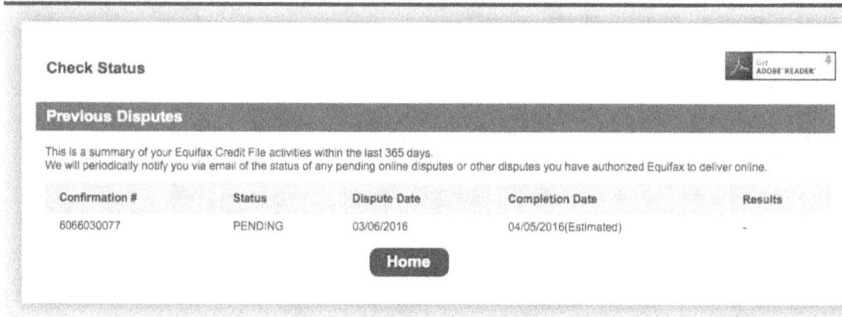

I highly recommend that you check your credit at least once a year and before a major purchase or before applying for a new job. It is best to avoid issues whenever possible.

To dispute other credit reports you can access Transunion and Experian at the following websites online.

Transunion Credit Dispute website

https://www.transunion.com/credit-disputes/dispute-your-credit

Experian Online Dispute

http://www.experian.com/disputes/main.html

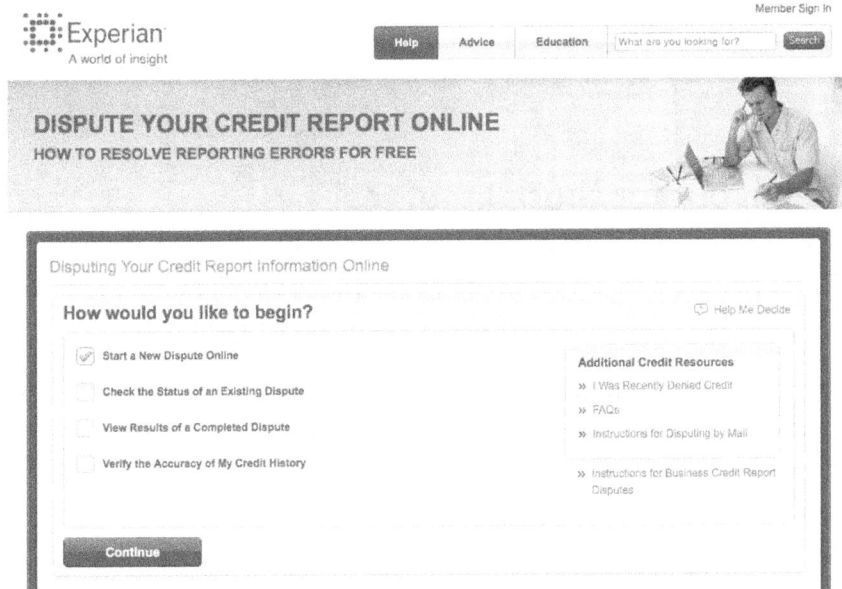

Experian has a similar interface to Equifax but more user friendly. It uses the same question and answer format.

Watch out for those Inquiries!

Inquiries are what happens when you apply for a new line of credit either indirectly or directly. They also appear when you complete a rental application to find a new apartment or sign up for a new utility service such as gas, electric, cell phone or internet. Be careful to not do this too often in a year! More than one or two inquiries may lower your overall credit FICO score. One great website with the inside scoop on factors that affect credit is MYFICO.com

http://www.myfico.com/crediteducation/creditchecks/inquiries.aspx

According to the MYFICO website the details on how inquiries affect one's credit score is summarized as thus:

Does applying for credit affect my FICO Scores?

FICO's research shows that opening several credit accounts in a short period of time represents greater credit risk. When the information on your credit report indicates that you have been applying for multiple new credit lines in a short period of time (as opposed to rate shopping for a single loan, which is handled differently as discussed below), your FICO Scores can be lower as a result.

How much will credit inquiries affect my score?

The impact from applying for credit will vary from person to person based on their unique credit histories. In general, credit inquiries have a small impact on one's FICO Scores. For most people, one additional credit inquiry will take less than five points off their FICO Scores. For perspective, the full range for FICO Scores is 300-850. Inquiries can have a greater impact if you have few accounts or a short credit history. Large numbers of inquiries also mean greater risk. Statistically, people with six inquiries or more on their credit reports can be up to eight times more likely to declare bankruptcy than people with no inquiries on their reports. While inquiries often can play a part in assessing risk, they play a minor part. Much more important factors for your scores are how timely you pay your bills and your overall debt burden as indicated on your credit report.

Source

> http://www.myfico.com/crediteducation/creditchecks/inquiries.aspx

In addition to tips on inquiries and your credit score, I highly recommend that you check out other helpful tips from the above

MYFICO website as it really is a hidden treasure trove of credit score goodness and financial tips!

Use less than you need on credit limit

Another key factor that affects your FICO credit score is how much of your credit limit is used each month. If you max out your credit cards at one time, that will drop your score quite a bit! Use only 1/3 of the limit. For example, if you have a Visa credit card with a $5000 limit, do not charge more than $1600 per month. By having several credit cards, you should not have an issue keeping at or below 1/3 of your total credit limit.

Pay credit cards in full every month

It should go without saying that you want to build and establish solid good credit for life. The key to this is to only use credit for what you can pay today and not buy impulse items that you cannot pay cash for today. As such, pay the cards in full every month. You need to do this to avoid nasty finance charges and maximize the cash back free money strategy. Only by doing this can you really make the free money strategy work out best for you. I once made a mistake and left a small balance on one of my cash back credit cards and ended up paying $20 fee that month. It cut into my free money balance. Even so, I still had $200 free cash back to me and made it work. BUT to avoid charges and get MORE FREE MONEY, pay each card off with diligence. Track charges with online banking to avoid delays and mistakes. I use my cash back credit card to buy gas and groceries which I would use my cash or bank debit card anyhow to buy on daily and weekly basis so I know that cash will be there each week to pay the card balance off completely. You can set email and phone text notifications to avoid forgetting when to pay the card off each week and month.

To back up my tips as to why you want to keep credit card balances under 1/3 of limit and pay off in full each month, Fair Isaac of MYFICO fame states that as well.

You can receive tips on credit score reporting and how to maintain good credit by visiting MYFICO at http://www.myfico.com/

Here is a good summary of credit card amounts owed and how credit score is affected.

http://www.myfico.com/CreditEducation/Amounts-Owed.aspx

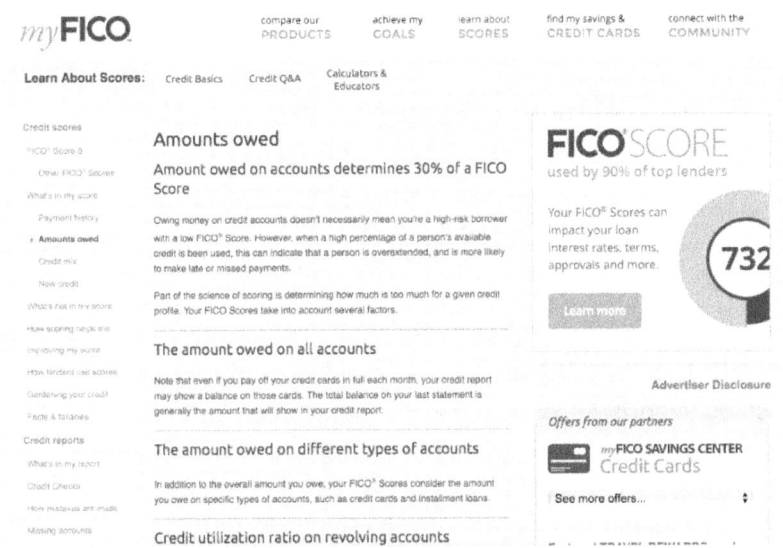

According to MYFICO the amounts owed per credit card account determine 30% of your FICO score! So if you owe a lot of your credit cards that will drag your FICO score down a lot.

Why Join a Credit Union?

I love my banks they treat me well as a premier customer. However, I recently joined a local credit union and love it! There are several great reasons to do so:

- Low Auto and Mortgage rates
- Good investment rates on CDs
- Free financial planning advice

When I joined the San Diego credit union, I opened a new certificate of deposit (CD) account. It gives me a 2% dividend and 1.9% interest rate against my deposit. In contrast, my bank only pays me a paltry 0.15% interest rate with no dividend on the CD that I have with them.

Also, if I ever want to buy a new or used car in the future, I can get a much lower loan rate than any bank. The credit union provides 1.65% auto loan rate for good credit versus 4% of the local banks! That is a lot of money folks!

Last but not least, free certified financial planners are provided at no cost to you as a credit union member. This is great help as I am not a financial planner and like to invest for the future.

Now that we covered how to build and keep good credit, lets discuss how to avoid bad mistakes with the program.

8 DON'T DO THIS!

By now you have learned some valuable money saving and free money back strategies. In this chapter, I am going to teach you how to avoid pitfalls and blunders that are common in using money and credit.

1. Bankruptcy

2. Forget to pay card each month

3. Overcharge past credit limit

4. Apply for too many cards at one time

5. Never apply as cosigner to credit

6. Avoid non member Bank ATM machines

Bankruptcy

I don't recommend bankruptcy in most cases. In fact, it can destroy your credit and employment prospects. The only time I recommend filing for bankruptcy is when you are in the most dire of all straits and then only after consulting with a bankruptcy lawyer. It stays on your credit report for **ten (10) years**!

9 PROMISING ENDS

In this chapter, I want to show you how to put together all of the different tips and techniques to maximize the free money savings that you learned earlier in the book. Just like a force multiplier when playing a video game or playing slot machines at a Casino in Vegas, we want to hedge our bets to triple the financial benefits and savings available to you with a few easy methods.

1. Buy using coupons with cash back credit card
2. Buy groceries and gas with cash back card.
3. Pay for vacations using bonus travel or cash back credit cards
4. Use a travel card that avoids foreign transaction fees
5. Build credit rating
6. Save like a miser!
7. Invest wisely

REMEMBER THE POWER OF THE COUPON!

Buy products on sale using store coupons and your cash back credit card! Sounds obvious but you would be surprised that few folks use coupons or are too embarrassed to whip out a two for one dinner special at a local Thai or Indian restaurant. Don't feel cheap it is common sense and will show your friends and family how wise you are when it comes to stretching the dollars. Every week usually on Wednesdays at least here in San Diego the main grocery chains have double coupon savings on produce, meat and frozen food goods. That is the golden time to stock up on food and save double at same time.

I always use my cash back credit cards to also buy groceries and save a lot that way. As an alternative, you can apply for a gas credit card to receive the discount but I find having a single go to card to be more convenient and easier to manage my budget and track my spending each week and month. Use whatever works best for your own situation.

TRAVEL CREDIT CARDS FOR VACATIONS

I love to travel! Unfortunately, airline fees and hotel costs have soared in years. Flying 15+ hours to an overseas paradise or that European vacation in coach or economy class stinks! It flat out sucks and is a painful ordeal best avoided. However, first class or international business tickets cost a small fortune these days. In fact, when I traveled to Switzerland for work recently, I wanted to upgrade until the Swiss Air agent blankly told me it would be another ten thousand bucks one way! So, I suffered a painful 14 hour flight in coach to Zurich and back. Since it was work I did not complain. However, when I took a vacation a few years back to South America, I had lot of time to plan. So, I booked online a red eye international business flight and guess what? It only cost me $500 more for a rountrip first class and international business ticket than economy! I loved it. Pay for these on cash back or travel perks credit cards that I told you all about in the beginning of this book. I funded my entire vacation this way in fact.

AVOID FOREIGN TRANSACTION FEES

One nasty surprise that hit me recently was foreign transaction fees on my trip to Zurich. Unfortunately since it was a last minute trip, I did not have the time to really plan it for work. I paid a lot in foreign transaction fees to withdraw money from the Swiss ATM machines. I did some research afterwards to discover this could have been avoided. Definitely get a credit card that avoids foreign transaction fees. It will save you hundreds of dollars if you do a lot of international travel! For a complete list go to www.creditcards.com and also www.nerdwallet.com for complete rundowns.

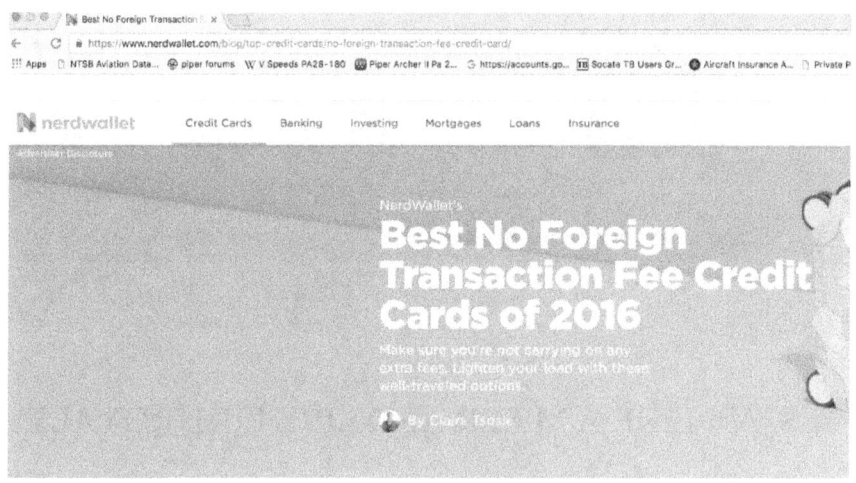

I like both financial credit card analysis websites as they provide tons of detailed information that you can review at your leisure.

Here is one such card that I can recommend:

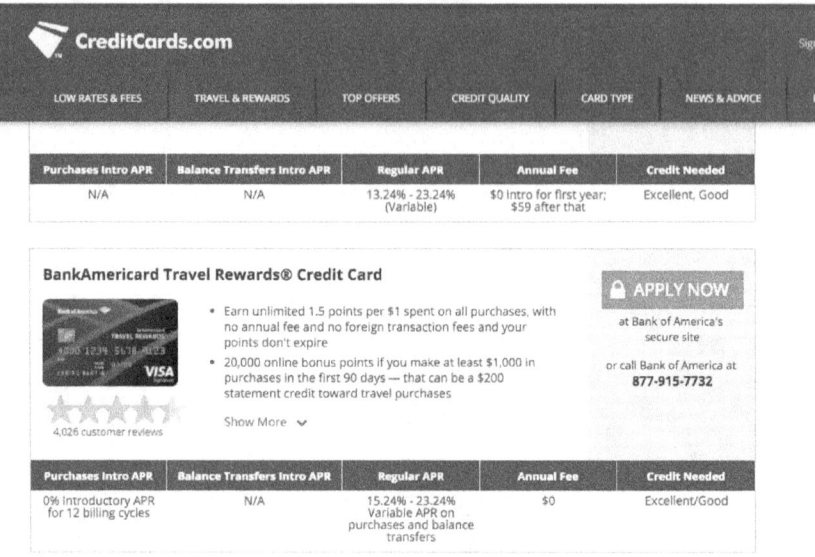

Purchases Intro APR	Balance Transfers Intro APR	Regular APR	Annual Fee	Credit Needed
N/A	N/A	13.24% - 23.24% (Variable)	$0 Intro for first year; $59 after that	Excellent, Good

BankAmericard Travel Rewards® Credit Card

APPLY NOW

at Bank of America's secure site

or call Bank of America at **877-915-7732**

- Earn unlimited 1.5 points per $1 spent on all purchases, with no annual fee and no foreign transaction fees and your points don't expire
- 20,000 online bonus points if you make at least $1,000 in purchases in the first 90 days — that can be a $200 statement credit toward travel purchases

Show More ⌄

4,026 customer reviews

Purchases Intro APR	Balance Transfers Intro APR	Regular APR	Annual Fee	Credit Needed
0% Introductory APR for 12 billing cycles	N/A	15.24% - 23.24% Variable APR on purchases and balance transfers	$0	Excellent/Good

SAVE LIKE A MISER AND LIVE LIKE ROYALTY!

With the holiday season and tight finances, many folks are in stressed out conditions and bad moods. I wrote this book to help cure that pain. Applying the valuable inside tips and tricks from earlier will allow you to experience real financial freedom at warp speed! Now I must admit that living frugally can yield serious dividends. Instead of eating fast food garbage daily, I shop at places like Trader Joes and buy healthy tasty meals that take minutes to prepare at half the cost of the swill served at McDonald or Taco Bell.

KEY TO SUCCESS: BUILD THAT CREDIT RATING!

Earlier I talked about why credit rating is so key to financial success. I walked you through the ins and outs of the mysterious FICO system and no folks, FICO is not where you take your car for an oil change. By watching credit carefully and following good credit management steps that I discussed you can open many doors to lucrative financial opportunities. Also you will always get the prime lowest finance rates should you ever decide to buy a home or finance a new luxury car. In my case, I have top tier credit and if I need a new car can easily get the lowest rate or best mortgage rate for a home loan. It also is key for business. Employers and potential investors will look into your credit history for top jobs and business opportunities. If they see a pattern of financial issues they will not give you consideration for high paying jobs. Trust me on this!

INVEST WISELY!

Once you have reaped money saved, I recommend that you fund a 401k, IRA or similar investment account right away. First, speak to a free financial advisor for guidance as I am not a CPA or certified financial planner and cannot give specific guidance in these areas. My CPA accountant saves me thousands a year in taxes and his fee is well worth his weight in gold! Likewise my financial planner helps a lot to decide how to park extra money for best future growth. I also have a good lawyer for difficult transaction advise such as real estate and so forth. Assemble your core team of these key advisers and you will be far more successful. In fact, President-elect and billionaire real estate mogul Donald Trump has a top notch advisory team. While I am not nearly as wealthy as Trump is, I do have my team of planners that earn the fees to save my hard earned money. Talk to family, friends, do research and you can build your very own A-team as well toward financial victory. Another reason for credit unions is the many free advisors that can help you plan the future without huge fees.

Conclusion

Well we have come to our end of your journey toward financial success. Hopefully you are rewarded by applying the many money saving tips in this guide. Visit my blog as well for future money saving tips and more. I wish you great success in your future!

10 STRATEGY CARD

Dear Readers:

Use this cheat card to internalize and master the free money now tips:

1. Obtain credit reports and credit scores for FREE
   http://www.annualcreditrport.com
2. Review credit reports and fix errors
3. Open a cash back credit card
4. Open a new bank account with free cash back offer
5. Use cash back credit card for groceries, gas, etc.
6. Pay off credit card in full before balance is due each month
7. Repeat steps five and six
8. Enjoy lots of free money now!

I also would love to hear your success stories and personal victories in using these strategies. Please spread the word and share the gift of wealth with others!

ABOUT THE AUTHOR

Ben Prusinski is a computer database engineer, pilot, scuba diver and lover of life's great adventures. He has traveled the world in style on a budget and enjoys making new friends in new places and experiences.